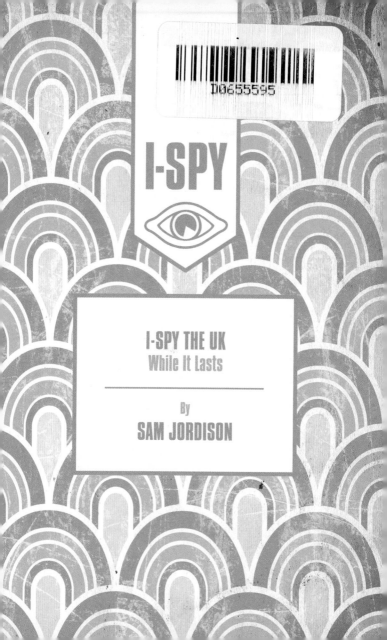

D0655595

I-SPY

I-SPY THE UK
While It Lasts

By
SAM JORDISON

HarperCollins*Publishers*
1 London Bridge Street
London SE1 9GF

www.harpercollins.co.uk

First published by HarperCollins*Publishers* 2016

10 9 8 7 6 5 4 3 2 1

© Sam Jordison 2016
Designed by Alexandra Allden © HarperCollins*Publishers* 2016

Sam Jordison asserts the moral right to be identified as
the author of this work

A catalogue record of this book is available from the
British Library

ISBN 978-0-00-822067-9

Printed and bound in Spain

MIX
Paper from
responsible sources
www.fsc.org **FSC™ C007454**

FSC™ is a non-profit international organisation established to promote the
responsible management of the world's forests. Products carrying the FSC
label are independently certified to assure consumers that they come from
forests that are managed to meet the social, economic and ecological needs
of present and future generations, and other controlled sources.

Find out more about HarperCollins and the environment at
www.harpercollins.co.uk/green

The I-SPY concept is simple. It's like the 'I spy with my little eye' game, only instead of all the tedious stuff about 'something beginning with', there are pictures and descriptions and genuine opportunities to use your sleuthing skills to discover interesting things. And laugh at them. It will greatly improve your thus far ignorant life.

The United Kingdom of Wales, England, Scotland and Northern Ireland isn't very united anymore. Great Britain isn't very great. Or so say wrong-headed doubters who want to talk us down! But where else can you see men in kilts, weirdly neat gardens and aggressively jovial village fetes? Nowhere else. And this guide helps you add to these great joys by awarding you points for seeing them. Isn't that the pip?

You earn a score every time you spot something pictured in this book. It's great fun to add up your scores and know that you're doing better than your friends and family.

When your score totals over 250 you're allowed to call yourself an I-SPY Stalwart, second-class honours.

When your score totals over 500, you can maybe even think about applying for UK residency.

If you score less than 250, you're a failure and we don't even feel sorry for you.

Chief I-SPY, LONDON

The Queue Jumper

An extremely rare sight in Britain. If you see one, you get a really wizard I-SPY score of 50 points.

I-SPYed on .... Score

at .... ⑤⓪

If someone in the queue says, 'You do know that there's a queue here, don't you?', take another 10 points.

I-SPYed on .... Score

at .... ①⓪

If someone in the queue says, 'Sorry, but you do know there's a queue here,' you've reached Peak Britain. Collect an extra 20 points.

I-SPYed on .... Score

at .... ②⓪

The Englishman

The Englishman is lonely and afraid because he's gone north of the border and none of the Scottish nationalists like him. Now he knows how it feels.

I-SPYed on .... Score

at .... (30)

Tacsi Sign

In Wales, taxis have two signs – one reading 'taxi' and one reading 'tacsi' – to help Welsh people who are confused by the letter 'x'.

I-SPYed on .... **Score**

at .... (10)

Pwll
Swimm

TACSI
TAXIS

Leisure Centre

This leisure centre was paid for with European money.
It has a fully equipped gym, indoor football pitches,
a swimming pool with a slide and a wave machine,
and it has closed.

I-SPYed on .... Score

at .... (20)

The Union Jack

The Union Jack is the united flag of England, Scotland, Wales and Northern Ireland. I know! Make sure you record your I-SPY points before it disappears entirely.

I-SPYed on .... **Score**

at .... **(20)**

See a Union Jack anywhere at all in Scotland.

I-SPYed on .... **Score**

at .... **(50)**

Fadge

This is a food often found in Northern Ireland, not a euphemism. It's a special kind of potato cake. That isn't a euphemism either. Wash your filthy mind out.

I-SPYed on .... **Score**

at .... **(20)**

Pub Bore

This jolly fellow loves a convivial pint with his friends
and you'll sometimes also spot him having a crafty fag
outside the pub. You'll know you've found him if you
hear him calling the landlord 'mein host' and making
off-colour jokes about current political hot potatoes.
He'll tell you that we can't know whether climate is
actually driven by carbon dioxide emissions. And he'll
blame the banking collapse on bad government policy
rather than greed. Make sure you leave the room before
he starts lying about Europe.

I-SPYed on .... **Score**

at .... (**30**)

The Bagpiper

The bagpiper can be seen on the streets of most Scottish towns at lunchtime, busking for coins. American tourists love him because for them he conjures up true Scotland: glens and lochs and dark, brooding mountains. Locals love him because his instrument reflects the sounds inside their heads: a long, loud, high-pitched screaming.

I-SPYed on .... Score

at .... (**20**)

If you see whatever it is that the bagpiper is hiding under his kilt, don't come running and complaining to me. I don't sanction looking at all.

I-SPYed on .... Score

at .... (**-50**)

The Houses of Parliament

The Houses of Parliament are split into two sections.
The House of Commons is where our elected
representatives gather to lie and jeer at each other.
The House of Lords is where old men go for a nice
quiet nap.

I-SPYed on .... Score

at .... (20)

Spot an actual politician on the grass outside
Parliament avoiding giving straight answers to a
TV presenter's questions.

I-SPYed on .... Score

at .... (20)

See a member of the public making rude signs behind
the politician's back for 30 extra points.

I-SPYed on .... Score

at .... (30)

The Leek

The Welsh national symbol is the leek. You'll see it on signs, and on some days schoolchildren will pin pretend leeks onto their uniform. This didn't make any sense before Brexit, either.

I-SPYed on .... Score

at .... (20)

You may also spot lots of daffodils. This is because the Welsh have two national symbols based on local fauna. Isn't that greedy?

I-SPYed on .... Score

at .... (20)

ffrwythau, llysiau,
blodau.

siop y gor

J. WILLI

Taps-aff

These young people have taken their shirts off! If you see someone doing the same, you'll know you've arrived in Scotland on a very special day: the one day in the entire year on which it's sunny enough for young men to remove their upper-body garments.

I-SPYed on.. Score

at .... (100)

In the evening, you may see some of the same young men, lobster-red and passed out on park benches. Score 10 I-SPY points.

I-SPYed on.. Score

at .... (10)

Village Fete

You'll see all sorts of interesting things at the
village fete!

Look out especially for the nice lady at the cake stall who
sells fondant fancies, angel cakes, rich fruitcake, brightly
coloured biscuits and thinks dark, terrible thoughts about
her neighbours and their thriving rhododendrons.

If you're very lucky, you may also see a maypole.
Back in the 17th century, the philosopher Thomas
Hobbes explained maypoles as follows: 'The Heathens
had also their *Aqua Lustralis*, that is to say, *Holy Water*...
They had their *Bacchanalia*; and we have our *Wakes*,
answering to them... They their Procession of *Priapus*;
we our fetching in, erection, and dancing about *Maypoles*.' Priapus was a Greek god, famous for the size and
visibility of his member. Which is worth thinking about
if you do I-SPY a maypole dance. That's right. You'll be
watching dancers tie ribbons around an eight-foot-high
penis. Isn't that just wizard?

I-SPYed on .... **Score**

at ....   (30)

Crisp Sandwiches

In Northern Ireland you'll see an unusually large number of crisp sandwiches. The people have endured more than their share of hard times. So they aren't afraid of carbohydrates and they don't mind showing it.

I-SPYed on .... Score

at .... (10)

The most popular crisps in Northern Ireland are Tayto crisps and they're made in a castle. Flavours include Curry, Ulster Fry and Vegetable Roll. It's impossible to imagine what those actually taste like, and you're not advised to find out. But you do get 10 extra I-SPY points for spotting them.

I-SPYed on .... Score

at .... (10)

Boy Racer

Boy Racers can be found throughout the UK. They make a lot of noise and they're a danger to pedestrians. But try not to feel too annoyed, because the faster a Boy Racer drives, the less likely it is that he has anywhere to go, and so he inadvertently provides a huge, all-encompassing metaphor for, well, everything.

I-SPYed on .... **Score**

at .... (**20**)

St George's Cross

This is the national flag of England. It is inadvisable to assume that people who wave it around are racist. They maybe just really like the England football team. The fact that you're likely to see a great many more of these flags if you go I-SPYing outside of metropolitan areas is merely a coincidence.

I-SPYed on .... Score

at .... (20)

See a St George's Cross that isn't being waved by an angry, bald white man for an extra 50 I-SPY points.

I-SPYed on .... Score

at .... (50)

Curtain Twitcher

Many houses in England have pretty, frilly net curtains on the windows. The owners enjoy hiding behind them while they check to see which of their neighbours are having affairs and make sure that there are no foreigners walking down the street. Look closely and you'll see the curtains move. Smashing!

I-SPYed on .... Score

at .... (20)

Did you see the Twitcher before the Twitcher saw you? Give yourself an extra 100 I-SPY points! This is one of the hardest spies in the book.

I-SPYed on .... Score

at .... (100)

Sunday Morning Car Cleaner

In suburbia you can get extra I-SPY points if you see a man furiously washing his car. Best spotted on a Sunday, the car cleaner can be seen with a power hose, buckets, chamois leather and a stern expression. Look closely and you'll see that there is actually no dirt on the car. The aim isn't to clean. The man is trying to wipe away the sadness from his life. He'll be there all day.

I-SPYed on .... Score

at .... (20)

Spot the Sunday morning car cleaner boring the dirtbox off everyone once he's transmogrified into the pub bore (see page 16) later in the week and take 30 extra points.

I-SPYed on .... Score

at .... (30)

Buckfast Drinker

Also known as 'commotion lotion', 'wreck the hoose joos', 'trampagne' and 'loopy joos', Buckfast is made by Benedictine monks in Devon, but almost exclusively drunk on the streets of Scotland. Thanks to its potent combination of caffeine, alcohol and mysteriously invigorating 'tonic', Buckfast has been linked to thousands of crimes and visits to A&E.

I-SPYed on .... **Score**

at .... (20)

The Finger Pointer

The English love to point the finger! Sometimes you'll
see people pointing at birds or interesting things by the
roadside. But most times they'll be pointing at people
they disapprove of. Make sure you aren't one of them.

People in the finger pointer's firing line might be
those who voice uncomfortable truths about metric
measurements just making more sense than pounds and
ounces. Or those trying to do Britain down by talking
about financial inequality. Some people don't even
know all the words to the national anthem and take
long, decadent holidays in France. These people are not
patriots and might even receive a stern finger wagging.

I-SPYed on .... Score

at ....   (20)

If you see a finger wagger, score 20 points.

I-SPYed on .... Score

at ....   (20)

If you wag the finger yourself, score 50 points.

I-SPYed on .... Score

at ....   (50)

The Iron Throne

The Iron Throne is the throne upon which the King of the Andals and the First Men sits. It's forged from swords. It's not real, but it's just about the most popular tourist attraction in the UK. Meanwhile, *Game of Thrones* now employs more people than the Civil Service in Northern Ireland. Winter is coming.

I-SPYed on .... **Score**

at .... $\boxed{50}$

The Coal Mines

British coal mines once fuelled the world. They fired the Industrial Revolution. They kept Britain's planes in the air and boats on the sea during the Second World War. For generations they gave communities work, cohesion and pride. They have closed.

I-SPYed on .... Score

at .... (20)

Titanic Museum

Belfast is renowned for building a gigantic ship that sank on its maiden voyage, costing more than 1500 people their lives. Yay!

I-SPYed on .... **Score**

at .... (20)

The Deep-fried Mars Bar

Go into a Scottish chip shop and you'll see people
covering Mars bars in batter, throwing them into deep-fat
fryers and serving them to grown men and women.
And tourists too. But don't be one of them. We need
our spies healthy and mobile.

I-SPYed on .... Score

at .... (30)

THE CARRON FISH BAR

(FORMERLY THE HAVEN)

BIRTHPLACE OF THE WORLD FAMOUS
DEEP FRIED MARS BAR

The Loch Ness Monster

Come off it!

I-SPYed on .... Score

at .... (150)

Honourable Rank of
NEW SPY
—
Awarded to

....

from

....

....

(FULL NAME AND ADDRESS HERE)

has become an acceptable citizen. This person has
demonstrated vigilance and diligence and earned
the Honourable Rank of New Spy.

First-class Honours
1000 POINTS - EXTRA MERIT

NOW ENCOURAGE YOUR FRIENDS AND NEIGHBOURS TO JOIN IN. OR ELSE.